Published in 2014 by The Rosen Publishing Group, Inc.
29 East 21st Street, New York, NY 10010

Photo Credits: **KEY** tl=top; tc=top center; tr=top right; cl=center left; c=center; cr=center right; bl=bottom left; bc=bottom center; br=bottom right; bg=background

CBT = Corbis; DT = Dreamstime; GI = Getty Images; iS = istockphoto.com; PDCD = PhotoDisc; PECD = PhotoEssentials; SH = Shutterstock; TPL = photolibrary.com

front cover iS; bg SH; **1**c iS; **4–5**c GI; **7**bc iS; **8**bg iS; **9**bg, cr iS; **10**bc CBT; cl iS; **12–13**bg iS; **13**br, cr, tr SH; **14**c CBT; bg SH; **14–15**bg TPL; **15**cr iS; bg SH; **16**bc, bl, c iS; **16–17**bc, bg iS; **17**bl iS; **18**tr DT; tc iS; **18–19**bg iS; **19**c, cl, tc DT; tl, tr iS; **20–21**cr GI; **21**tr iS; **24**bl, cl, CBT; tl TPL; **24–25** tc CBT; bg iS; **25**br, cr, tr iS; tc TPL; **26**tl iS; bg SH; **26–27**bg SH; **27**tr SH; **28**cl CBT; bc PDCD; **28–29**bc PDCD; tc, bg SH; **29**br, tr DT; **30**br iS; bg, cr PECD; **31**br, br, br DT

All illustrations copyright Weldon Owen Pty Ltd except **8–9** bg Dr. Mark A. Garlick

Weldon Owen Pty Ltd
Managing Director: Kay Scarlett
Creative Director: Sue Burk
Publisher: Helen Bateman
Senior Vice President, International Sales: Stuart Laurence
Vice President Sales North America: Ellen Towell
Administration Manager, International Sales: Kristine Ravn

Publisher's Cataloging Data

Coupe, Robert.
Earth's treasures: rocks and minerals / by Robert Coupe.
p. cm. — (Discovery education: earth and space science)
Includes index.
ISBN 978-1-4777-6170-0 (library binding) — ISBN 978-1-4777-6172-4 (pbk.) —
ISBN 978-1-4777-6173-1 (6-pack)
1. Rocks — Juvenile literature. 2. Minerals — Juvenile literature. I. Coupe, Robert. II. Title.
QE432.2 C68 2014
552.0078 —d23

Manufactured in the United States of America

CPSIA Compliance Information: Batch #W14PK2: For Further Information contact Rosen Publishing, New York, New York at 1-800-237-9932

EARTH AND SPACE SCIENCE

EARTH'S TREASURES
ROCKS AND MINERALS

ROBERT COUPE

PowerKiDS
press

New York

Contents

Earth's Place in Space

With its vast oceans and masses of air, planet Earth seems enormous. But it is just one of eight planets in our solar system, all orbiting the much larger Sun. The Sun is just one star in hundreds of billions in our galaxy, and this galaxy is one of billions we can see in the universe.

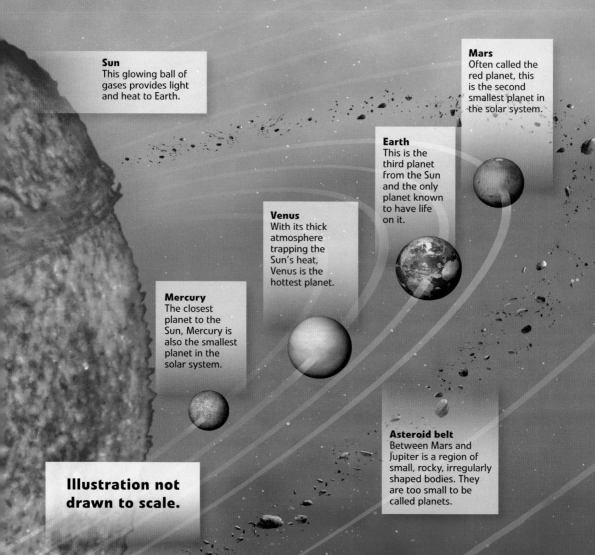

Sun
This glowing ball of gases provides light and heat to Earth.

Mars
Often called the red planet, this is the second smallest planet in the solar system.

Earth
This is the third planet from the Sun and the only planet known to have life on it.

Venus
With its thick atmosphere trapping the Sun's heat, Venus is the hottest planet.

Mercury
The closest planet to the Sun, Mercury is also the smallest planet in the solar system.

Asteroid belt
Between Mars and Jupiter is a region of small, rocky, irregularly shaped bodies. They are too small to be called planets.

Illustration not drawn to scale.

Uranus
Compared to all the other planets, Uranus is tipped on its side.

Saturn
This planet is surrounded by an icy ring system, but is otherwise quite similar to Jupiter.

Neptune
Neptune is the farthest planet from the Sun, has icy moons, and is surrounded by a series of dark rings.

Jupiter
Bigger than all the other planets combined, Jupiter is the largest planet in the solar system.

FORMATION OF THE SOLAR SYSTEM

Scientists believe the solar system was formed about 4.6 billion years ago, when a cloud of gas and dust in outer space was disturbed, possibly by an exploding star.

1 Shrinking cloud
A cloud of gas started to shrink under its own gravity.

2 Spinning disk
As it shrank, the cloud heated up, flattened out, and started to spin, forming a gigantic disk.

4 Formation
These attracted to one another, forming even larger objects. The Sun formed at the center, and planets gradually formed around it.

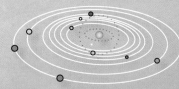

3 Combined objects
Particles inside the disk started to combine, forming small Moon-like objects.

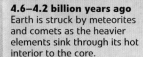

4.6–4.2 billion years ago
Earth is struck by meteorites and comets as the heavier elements sink through its hot interior to the core.

4.2–3.8 billion years ago
Lava flowing from craters cool and form Earth's crust. Oceans fill with water from volcanoes and comets.

Watery world
From space, Earth appears blue and white. The blue is because more than 70 percent of its surface is made up of oceans and seas. The white is from the water in the form of clouds and ice.

Early Earth

Earth began to form about 4.6 billion years ago from the same cloud of gas and dust that formed our Sun and the rest of the solar system. Over time, gravity slowly drew gas, ice, dust, and small rocks together to form the planets and moons we now see.

Meteorite effect

All of the planets and their moons have been struck by asteroids millions of times. When we look at our Moon, we can see the huge craters caused by meteorites and comets that collided with its surface over billions of years. The lack of atmosphere or tectonic plates means these craters will never disappear.

METEORITE IMPACT

Asteroids today can sometimes be deflected out of the asteroid belt and eventually collide with a planet, creating a crater whose size depends on the mass of the object.

1 Approaching asteroid
This becomes red-hot from friction and partially melts in the atmosphere of the planet or moon.

2 Ball of fire
This takes about four seconds to descend from 50 miles (80 km), before striking and vaporizing surface rocks.

3 Impact
A cloud of vaporized rock and white-hot fragments sprays into the air.

4 Cooling vapor
Vapor cools and condenses into rocks, scattering over a wide area. Super-hot rocks explode from underground, forming a hill at the crater's center.

5 The crater
A circular shape is formed no matter what direction the asteroid comes from.

Elements inside Earth

Although we cannot drill deep enough to fully learn about Earth's interior, rocks and minerals from other planets give an idea of what makes up our own inner planet.

Crust

- Silicon 58%
- Aluminum 16%
- Iron 8%
- Magnesium 4%
- Calcium 7%
- Sodium 3%
- Potassium 2%
- Other 2%

Mantle

- Silicon 45%
- Magnesium 41%
- Iron 8%
- Aluminum 3%
- Calcium 2%
- Other 1%

Core

- Iron 84%
- Nickel 6%
- Other 10%

Inside Earth

Earth is made up of several layers that developed when it was still a ball of molten rock. If we were to travel to the center of Earth, we would first have to pass through the thin, rocky crust. Next, we would journey through the deep mantle, which is made of flexible but solid rock. Passing through the boiling-hot liquid outer core, we would reach Earth's inner core, which is a red-hot, solid ball of iron and nickel.

Olivine
Fragments of Earth's mantle, which are carried to the surface by volcanic eruptions, are called olivine.

Earth's layers

Most of Earth is solid, but at its center is a molten outer core. Inside this is a solid inner core. The temperature in the inner core is estimated to be 8,000°F (4,000°C).

Crust
This thin layer of rock covering Earth can be between 3 and 45 miles (5 and 70 km) thick.

Asthenosphere
This layer of soft, partly molten rock is about 125 miles (200 km) thick.

Mantle
The upper mantle is made up of supple, moving rock, while the deeper mantle is solid rock.

Outer core
Made of iron and nickel, this is fully liquid.

Inner core
This is a red-hot, solid ball of iron and nickel.

The asthenosphere, on which Earth's crust floats, moves at rates of up to 4 inches (10 cm) each year.

Convection currents
When fluids warm up and cool down, they flow around in cycles called convection currents. These currents move the plates of rock that form Earth's crust.

Changing Rocks

Rocks are pushed up by tectonic forces, then eroded by wind and rain. When molten rock cools, igneous rocks are formed. The debris from eroded rocks collects as layers of sediment. These are pressed together to form sedimentary rocks. Intense heat and pressure can transform these layers into metamorphic rocks.

Rocks on the move

For nearly 5 billion years, rocks underneath us have been moving. The rock cycle is a very slow process. Molten rock erupts from volcanoes, erodes, and reforms as new rocks. Eventually, it is pulled back deep underground.

Rocks, mud, and sand are deposited at river deltas and on the ocean floor.

River and ocean deposits form layers of sedimentary rock.

Ocean crust

Mantle

Tectonic plate movement pulls sediment deep underground.

Types of rocks
It takes millions of years for rocks to form and change. There are three types of rocks that can be found on Earth.

Rock is eroded and swept away.

Molten rock cools and hardens, forming igneous rocks.

Continental crust

Underground heat and pressure form metamorphic rocks.

Igneous rocks
When molten rock solidifies after erupting from a volcano, igneous rocks are formed. Examples include granite, basalt, and flint.

Sedimentary rocks
These are formed when igneous rocks are eroded to form layers of sediment. Fossils are often found in this layer. Examples are limestone, chalk, and sandstone.

Metamorphic rocks
These are made up of igneous and sedimentary rocks that have been transformed by intense heat and pressure. Examples are slate, marble, and quartzite.

Rocks and Minerals

All rocks are made from minerals. Rocks are the materials that mountains, cliffs, and the soil are made of. Even sand and clay are types of rock that are made from tiny particles. The processes that shape rocks to form landscapes can take thousands or even millions of years.

Rocks

Rocks are used to build houses, bridges, and many other man-made objects. Materials can be cut from large or small stones, and sometimes processed to make bricks. Cement is a common building material that is made from sedimentary rocks. Rocks can be treated with heat and chemicals to produce glass and other ceramics. For millions of years, people have used rocks to make tools and weapons for hunting and survival.

Minerals

Minerals are naturally occurring substances found in the ground that are not part of an animal or a plant. The minerals inside a rock usually form small crystal grains that are locked together to form a hard, solid object. Some minerals are single elements, such as gold and sulfur, while others are compounds of two or more elements, such as silicates.

Crystals

A crystal is an organized group of atoms or molecules. Crystals can take on different properties and shapes. For example, sugar crystals are oblong and slanted at the ends, while salt crystals are cubic. Crystals have many different uses. Diamonds, emeralds, rubies, and sapphires have been treasured as precious jewels for thousands of years, while tiny vibrating crystals are used in radios and clocks.

Magical Minerals

Scientists have identified more than 2,500 different minerals, many of which are very rare. Most minerals can be found in Earth's crust. Some minerals, such as clay minerals, form at the surface. Some form at shallow depths, while others form deep within Earth's crust. Mineral deposits come in all shapes and sizes, depending on where and how the mineral was concentrated.

Minerals can also be identified by streak, luster, gravity, fracture, and crystal form.

Color identification
Often the most striking feature of a mineral is color. The difficulty with color is that it is not a very reliable method of identifying a mineral because of impurities. For example, diamonds and quartz are often found in a wide range of colors.

Rhodochrosite
Rosy pink

Malachite
Dark green

Sulfur
Bright yellow

Fluorite
Purple

Fluorite
Yellow

Fluorite
Green

Amethyst

Opal

Pyrite

Transparency

How well we can see objects through a mineral is known as transparency. Many minerals, such as quartz, are transparent when in a pure state. Others, such as moonstone, are semitransparent. Translucent minerals let a small amount of light through, while opaque ones allow no light at all.

Quartz
Transparent

Moonstone
Semitransparent

Chrysoprase
Translucent

Malachite
Opaque

Barite

Mohs scale of hardness

This scale of mineral hardness uses 10 minerals, ranging from the softest to the hardest, to help determine the hardness of other minerals. For example, by scratching quartz against a mystery mineral so that it leaves a mark, we know the unknown mineral is softer than quartz.

1 Talc

2 Gypsum

2.5 Fingernail

3 Calcite

3.5 Copper coin

4 Fluorite

5 Apatite

5.5 Glass

6.5 Steel knife

6 Orthoclase

7 Quartz

8 Topaz

8.5 Emery board

9 Corundum

10 Diamond

Stunning Stones

To be called a precious gemstone, a mineral must be beautiful, durable, and rare. Some of the best-known precious gemstones are diamonds, rubies, sapphires, and emeralds. Amethyst was once referred to as precious but is no longer considered rare after large deposits were discovered in Brazil. Sulfur is not durable enough to be considered precious, and quartz is far too common to be labeled precious. One of the most prized precious stones is alexandrite, which is extremely rare and can change from green to red in differing light.

Durable diamonds

Made of pure carbon, diamonds are the hardest mineral of all. Diamonds were first discovered at least 2,000 years ago and were found mainly in rivers in India.

Diamonds
Many diamonds look clear. Most have a slight tinge of yellow, while less common colors include pink, green, blue, purple, and red, which is the rarest of all.

Rubies
When chromium mixes with corundum, the mineral appears red and is known as a ruby. Bloodred rubies are some of the rarest gems in the world.

BIRTHSTONES

Some believe birthstones are linked to the 12 gems in the breastplate of Aaron, the brother of Moses, which represent the 12 tribes of Israel. More recent associations link them with the 12 months of the year.

JANUARY
Garnet

FEBRUARY
Amethyst

MARCH
Aquamarine

APRIL
Diamond

MAY
Emerald

JUNE
Pearl

JULY
Ruby

AUGUST
Peridot

SEPTEMBER
Sapphire

OCTOBER
Opal

NOVEMBER
Topaz

DECEMBER
Turquoise

Tourmaline
This crystalline mineral is classified as a semiprecious gemstone. It comes in a variety of colors, the most common of which is black.

Making diamonds
For diamonds to form from pure carbon, extremely high pressure is needed. This can be found only about 90 miles (145 km) below the ground.

Emeralds
These are transparent forms of the mineral beryl. They are often colored green from traces of chromium.

Rising to the surface
Magma formed in the mantle moves up into the crust, bringing diamonds with it.

Sapphires
The most common color for sapphires is blue, but orange and yellow stones have also been found.

Exploding bubbles
As the magma nears the surface, gas bubbles form and the magma begins to boil, causing an explosion.

Garnet
These have been used since the Bronze Age and can be found in many colors. The rarest is the blue garnet.

On the surface
Broken rock and magma harden in the volcano's funnel. Erosion carries some of the diamonds to nearby rivers.

NORTH
AMERICA

EUROPE

ASIA

AFRICA

SOUTH
AMERICA

AUSTRALIA

Where in the world?
Diamonds come from countries where there were explosive volcanoes. Most emeralds are found in South America. Rubies and sapphires are often found in rivers.

KEY
 Diamonds
 Emeralds
 Sapphires
 Rubies

Igneous Rocks

These rocks are formed through the cooling and solidification of molten rock. Igneous rocks that form deep within Earth's crust at very high temperatures can take thousands of years to cool down. This causes the crystals to be much larger, such as in the case of granite. Igneous rocks formed on the surface cool down in a matter of hours. The crystals in these rocks can be microscopically small.

COLUMN FORMATION

Rock columns are the result of ancient remains of old volcanic cones and their lava flows. As the softer surrounding rock is eroded, large cathedral-like columns begin to emerge.

Cooling lava
The lava begins to cool and shrink as heat is lost to the air from its surface and to the ground from underneath.

Tension cracks
Tiny cracks begin to appear as tension increases over the cooling surface. The cracks begin to grow toward the hot center.

Complete columns
Columns form as the cracks from the top and bottom of the lava flow join up with each other in the center.

Basalt sands
This black beach, located at Dyrholaey in Iceland, gets its black sand from the basaltic lava in the surrounding area.

The Giant's Causeway

These amazing columns in Northern Ireland were formed when volcanic basalt erupted after the landmasses of Europe and North America split 60 million years ago. As the lava cooled, incredible hexagonal columns emerged, some as wide as 2 feet (60 cm) across.

FORMING A CANYON

Canyons are formed when water flows over a piece of land for millions of years. The water begins to cut deep into the rocks, forming canyons and gorges.

Pathways form
As sea levels fall or land rises, sedimentary rocks are exposed. Rivers and streams begin to cut narrow pathways through the land.

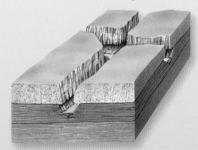

Land erodes
Land continues to erode as water cuts deeper into hard rock. As rivers reach softer layers, water digs underneath the harder rock.

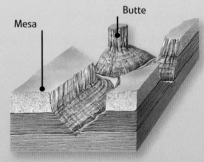

Butte

Mesa

Valleys widen
The water flowing underneath the hard rock causes the upper layers to collapse. Large mesas and small buttes are formed.

Sedimentary Rocks

Over millions of years, igneous rocks are weathered by forces of wind and water, and transform into small rock particles that are carried to the bottom of lakes and oceans. Slowly, the layer of sediment grows deeper and deeper, reaching depths of thousands of feet. The immense weight of all the sediment pushes downward on to lower layers with tremendous force. This process, combined with minerals that act like cement, bond the sediment together to form sedimentary rock.

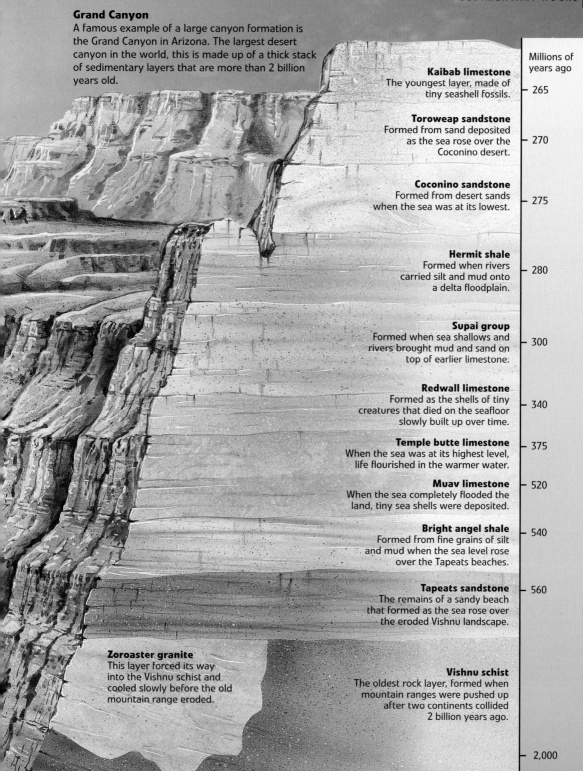

Grand Canyon
A famous example of a large canyon formation is the Grand Canyon in Arizona. The largest desert canyon in the world, this is made up of a thick stack of sedimentary layers that are more than 2 billion years old.

Millions of years ago

Kaibab limestone
The youngest layer, made of tiny seashell fossils.

— 265

Toroweap sandstone
Formed from sand deposited as the sea rose over the Coconino desert.

— 270

Coconino sandstone
Formed from desert sands when the sea was at its lowest.

— 275

Hermit shale
Formed when rivers carried silt and mud onto a delta floodplain.

— 280

Supai group
Formed when sea shallows and rivers brought mud and sand on top of earlier limestone.

— 300

Redwall limestone
Formed as the shells of tiny creatures that died on the seafloor slowly built up over time.

— 340

Temple butte limestone
When the sea was at its highest level, life flourished in the warmer water.

— 375

Muav limestone
When the sea completely flooded the land, tiny sea shells were deposited.

— 520

Bright angel shale
Formed from fine grains of silt and mud when the sea level rose over the Tapeats beaches.

— 540

Tapeats sandstone
The remains of a sandy beach that formed as the sea rose over the eroded Vishnu landscape.

— 560

Zoroaster granite
This layer forced its way into the Vishnu schist and cooled slowly before the old mountain range eroded.

Vishnu schist
The oldest rock layer, formed when mountain ranges were pushed up after two continents collided 2 billion years ago.

— 2,000

Metamorphic Rocks

These rocks form below Earth's surface, when heat and pressure are applied to either igneous rocks or sedimentary rocks. This heat and pressure "cook" the rocks and greatly change their structure. The rocks partially melt, which transforms their chemical composition so that the final rock is very different to the original rock. A common metamorphic rock is marble, which forms when heat and pressure are applied to limestone over thousands of years.

Metamorphic categories
Different types of metamorphic rocks can form depending on the pressure and heat applied to the rocks.

Phyllite
This type of layered metamorphic rock is primarily composed of quartz, sericite, mica, and chlorite.

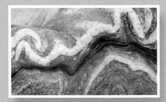

Amphibolite
Consisting mainly of hornblende amphibole, this is a dark-colored, heavy rock.

Gneiss
This medium- or coarse-grained metamorphic rock is common and widely distributed.

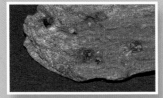

Schist
This coarse-grained metamorphic rock has a layered appearance.

Regional metamorphism
This begins when opposing forces on the tectonic plates squeeze a large area of land. The opposing force folds and crushes the rocks, creating various metamorphic rocks, depending on heat and pressure.

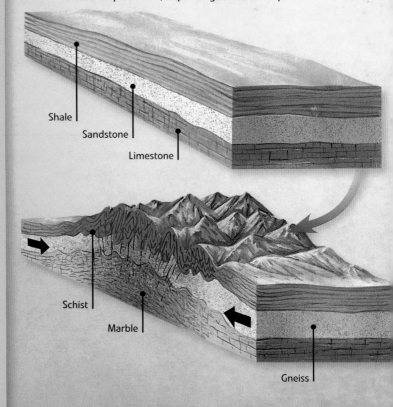

Shale

Sandstone

Limestone

Schist

Marble

Gneiss

Quartzite rocks
The quartzite rock structure in the Yellowstone Creek Basin, Utah, is striped with purple.

Mountain marvels
Giant mountain ranges, such as the Himalayas, contain metamorphic rocks that have formed over millions of years.

Contact metamorphism
This occurs when magma rises up through rock layers. The magma heats the surrounding stone and various metamorphic rocks are created, depending on the types of rocks present.

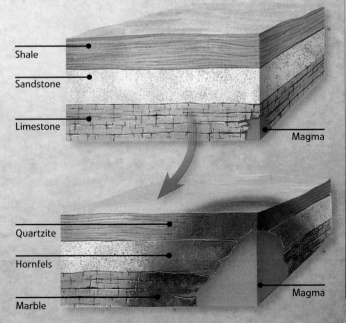

Shale

Sandstone

Limestone

Magma

Quartzite

Hornfels

Marble

Magma

METAMORPHIC USES
Metamorphic rocks have a variety of uses in everyday activities. They have been used in buildings, carvings, tools, and decorations.

Marble
The Taj Mahal in India was built using the metamorphic rock marble.

Jade
The metamorphic rock jade has been used in Chinese carvings for many centuries.

Lapis
This deep-blue metamorphic rock has been used in decorative artwork since ancient times.

Fascinating Fossils

Amber
Sometimes whole organisms can become trapped in the sticky resin of trees and are preserved intact. These wasps were not able to escape in time and became entombed for millions of years.

S ometimes, when an animal or plant dies, the remains are buried before they can be destroyed. If conditions are right, the remains get preserved as fossils. Fossils are the ancient remains or traces of animals, plants, and other organisms that have been preserved in Earth's crust. Fossils may be in the form of a shell, a bone, a tooth, a leaf, or even a footprint.

Unearthing layers
The oldest rock is found at the deepest layers and may contain traces of algae. In the layers above, more complex plants and animals can be found. Each layer can be assigned to different eras. Early life is found in Paleozoic-era rocks. Later life is found in Mesozoic-era rocks and more recent life in Cenzoic-era rocks.

Did You Know?
Fossils can range in age from 3.5 billion-year-old traces of microscopic algae to 10,000-year-old remains of animals preserved during the last ice age.

FOSSILIZATION
Dinosaur fossils are extremely rare. For a dinosaur to become a fossil, it had to be buried quickly before it decayed or was eaten by scavengers. Usually, only the hard bones and teeth of dinosaurs became fossilized. Sometimes dinosaur dung and footprints were fossilized.

70 million years ago
A giant, wet, sand dune collapsed on two clashing dinosaurs, trapping them under layers of sand. Their soft tissue rotted, however their skeletons were preserved.

Trilobite fossils

Trilobites were a type of anthropod, or hard-shelled marine animal, that lived about 250 million years ago, before dying out at the end of the Paleozoic era. Fossil records show thousands of different trilobite species.

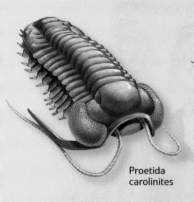

Proetida
carolinites

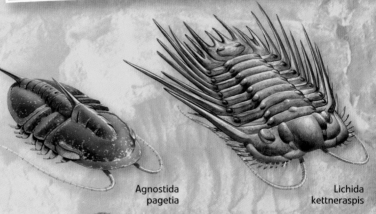

Agnostida
pagetia

Lichida
kettneraspis

40 million years ago
The skeletons were compressed under layers of rock, and groundwater chemicals transformed the bones into rock-hard fossils.

20,000 years ago
Movements in Earth's crust created new mountains that were partly worn down in the last ice age, bringing the fossils close to the surface.

Present day
Wind and water eroded surface rocks and the fossils were exposed. The slow, human process of extracting dinosaur fossils from the rock began.

Amazing Earth

Earth and the people who inhabit it have created some amazing structures over the years. These range from natural landmarks, such as the Great Barrier Reef in Australia and the Grand Canyon, to man-made marvels, such as the Hoover Dam and the Panama Canal, which joins the Atlantic and Pacific Oceans. Here are some famous spectacles on our planet.

Minerals in fireworks
Various natural minerals, such as iron, aluminum, and copper, are combined in fireworks to produce the beautiful range of colors we see during a firework display.

Cullinan diamond
The world's largest gem was found in a South African mine in 1905. The precious stones cut from the gem can be found among the British Crown Jewels.

Stonehenge
This monument was constructed more than 4,000 years ago in Wiltshire, England. For centuries, people have been trying to solve the mystery of how and why these giant stones were placed here.

Mount Rushmore
Between 1927 and 1941, 400 workers worked tirelessly to carve the heads of four US presidents into the cliff face on Mount Rushmore in South Dakota.

The Carlsbad Caverns
Over millions of years, running water hollowed out this limestone cave system in New Mexico. It is 37 miles (59.5 km) long and the world's largest subterranean chamber.

The Great Pyramid of Giza
This giant, man-made marvel in Egypt took thousands of workers 20 years to construct. It consists of more than 2.3 million limestone blocks and remained the tallest man-made structure in the world for 3,800 years!

Uluru
This sandstone formation in outback Australia stands 1,142 feet (348 m) high and measures 5.8 miles (9.4 km) in circumference. Uluru's appearance changes throughout the year, from bright red at sunset to silvery gray during the wet season.

Make Your Own Fossil

With a few simple items that you can find about the house, you can make a fossil imprint!

1 Place the parchment paper on the baking pan.

2 Fill the plastic container halfway with soil.

3 Slowly mix a little water with the soil until you get a thick, sticky mud you can shape by hand into a mold.

4 Place the fossil item into the center of the mud mold.

5 Place the mold onto the parchment paper to form a mud pie. Make sure the fossil item cannot be seen from the outside of the mud.

6 Put the baking pan outside in the sun or on a warm windowsill so the mud mold can dry and become solid.

7 When your mud mold is completely dry and hard, carefully break it open and your fossil will be revealed.

HINT
You can also try to make a fossil using your own handprint or footprint. Instead of using mud, you can also try clay or plaster.

Imagine finding a real fossil which has been buried for millions of years!

What you need:

- ☑ Parchment paper
- ☑ Flat metal baking pan
- ☑ Plastic container for mixing
- ☑ Soil
- ☑ Water
- ☑ Spoon for stirring
- ☑ Fossil item, such as a leaf, a small snail, a seashell, a piece of wood, or a nut in its shell

Glossary

asteroid
(AS-teh-royd)
A small, rocky, celestial body that orbits the Sun.

asthenosphere
(as-THEE-nus-feer)
The lower layer of Earth's crust.

atmosphere
(AT-muh-sfeer)
A layer of gases surrounding Earth that is retained by Earth's gravity.

comet (KAH-mit)
An object made of rock and ice that travels in long orbits around the Sun.

core (KOR)
The central region of a planet, star, or galaxy.

crater (KRAY-tur)
A hole caused by a comet or meteorite colliding with the surface of a planet or moon.

fracture (FRAK-chur)
The mark left on a mineral when it chips or breaks.

gravity (GRA-vih-tee)
The invisible force that pulls everything toward the center of a planet.

igneous (IG-nee-us)
Describes rock formed by the solidification of molten magma.

lava (LAH-vuh)
Molten rock that flows from a volcano during an eruption. It is formed in the interior of a planet.

luster (LUH-stur)
The glow of reflected light, especially on the surface of a mineral.

mantle (MAN-tul)
The interior region of a planet or other solid body that is below the crust and surrounds the core.

metamorphic
(meh-tuh-MOR-fik)
Describes rock altered by pressure and heat.

meteorite
(MEE-tee-uh-ryt)
A piece of stone or metal from space that collides with the surface of a moon or planet.

minerals (MIN-rulz)
Solid chemical substances that form within Earth and other planets. They are the building blocks of rocks.

molten (MOHL-ten)
Describes rock that is reduced to liquid by intense heat.

orbit (OR-bit)
The name for the path that one celestial object takes around another, larger celestial object.

sedimentary
(seh-duh-MEN-tuh-ree)
Describes rock formed from the buildup of sand, silt, and clay sediments.

solar system
(SOH-lur SIS-tum)
The Sun, together with the eight planets and all other celestial bodies that orbit the Sun.

star (STAR)
A ball of mostly hydrogen and helium gas that shines extremely brightly.

streak (STREEK)
The color of the fine powder that is obtained when a mineral is rubbed or scratched against a hard white surface.

transparency
(tranz-PER-en-see)
The state of being easy to see through.

Index

Websites

Due to the changing nature of Internet links, PowerKids Press has developed an online list of websites related to the subject of this book. This site is updated regularly. Please use this link to access the list:
www.powerkidslinks.com/disc/rocks/